The Secret Beginnings of Germany's Panzer Troops

Souvenir photo showing Panzer soldiers of Panzer Regiment 1 before the Daimler-Benz Grosstraktor on display at the Löberfeld Barracks in Erfurt.

Michael Scheibert

Schiffer Military/Aviation History
Atglen, PA

The 1917 model Ehrhardt Armored Road Vehicle. With 33 of them built, this was the most-used vehicle of its kind on the German side.

Photo Credits

Archives of:
- Wolfgang Fleischer
- Walter J. Spielberger
- Werner Haupt
- F. M. von Senger und Etterlin
- Kurt Kulke
- Horst Scheibert
- Horst Riebenstahl
- Karl-Theo Schleicher
- and the author

Translated from the German by Ed Force

Copyright © 1999 by Schiffer Publishing, Ltd.

Printed in China.
ISBN: 0-7643-0788-6

This book was originally published under the title,
Waffen Arsenal-Geheime Anfänge der deutschen Panzertruppe
by Podzun-Pallas Verlag.

We are interested in hearing from authors with book ideas on related topics.

Cover Picture

Cover artwork by Steve Ferguson, Colorado Springs, CO.

Published by Schiffer Publishing Ltd.
4880 Lower Valley Road
Atglen, PA 19310
Phone: (610) 593-1777
FAX: (610) 593-2002
E-mail: Schifferbk@aol.com
Please visit our web site catalog at www.schifferbooks.com
or write for a free catalog.
This book may be purchased from the publisher.
Please include $3.95 postage.
Try your bookstore first.

Foreword

The origin of the German Panzer troops was shaped for a long period of time by severe hindrances and opposition. As in Austria in 1911, so too in the German Reich in the following year, design drawings of a gun car, running on chain tracks, made by Oberleutnant Burstyn, were rejected by the Ministry of War. In Britain and France, though, experience had been gained by the end of 1914 from the unsuccessful and bloody battles around Flanders. Independently of each other, armored vehicles that proved to be usable were developed in both countries.

The further development of these vehicles, referred to in the British Army under the disguise name of "tank" and in the French Army as "char de combat", was carried on energetically in both countries.

They united the characteristics of the armored combat vehicle that apply to this day: firepower, mobility and armor protection. The British tanks, first used in small numbers and small groups, achieved only meager success in their first use in September 1916. After several subsequent uses, poorly directed in tactical terms, during the course of 1917, the unexpected mass application of British tanks during the battle of Cambrai on November 20, 1917 resulted in a German defeat there. Through them the old lesson was stressed again, that surprising the enemy is a decisive prerequisite for success. By using this new weapon, the Allies were able to overcome the sluggishness of positional war and gain the initiative. The Germans possessed some thirty captured British tanks, of the Mark IV type and fifteen German armored assault vehicles of Type A. 7. V., while the Allies had more than 2000 armored vehicles. On the German side there were never more than thirteen such vehicles in action at one time. The original scorn for this new weapon brought bitter results. Only at the beginning of 1918 were the first German A.7.V. armored assault vehicles delivered. In mid-1918 it was decided to begin the mass production of 800 light battle tanks. The Germans had missed their chance, for these vehicles never got into action. The development of the gigantic "K" large battle tank was given up even before the end of the war.

After the war ended, though, it was to be more than ten years before the German military leadership was finally able to build up its own Panzer troop.

In the Treaty of Versailles, the victorious powers issued a general ban on armored combat vehicles. This meant the end of the German Panzer troop of 1918.

As the only motorized troop remaining in the Reichswehr, there remained one truck unit (transport battalion) for each of the seven infantry divisions.

The creator of the Reichwehr, Generaloberst Hans von Seekt, followed the terms of the Treaty of Versailles scru-pulously, in order to give the Allies no reason to extend their stay in Germany. In order to assure a high level of training for the command of the 100,000-man army despite the limitations of the peace treaty, he formed the basis of a large modern army for officer training. Unlike other armies, he made sure that the service guidelines for the Reichswehr reflected mobile rather than positional warfare, and thus the "old stiffness" was overcome.

Thus he created an army of leaders and cadres, and at the same time made sure that this army, despite the weapons that were banned and therefore lacking, was trained for the tasks of a large army of the modern type.

"The motorization of the armies is one of the most important questions of military development. . . . The motor

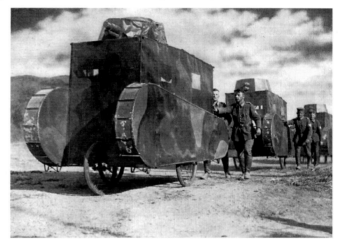

By the terms of the Treaty of Versailles, Germany was banned from building or owning armored combat vehicles. In the Reichswehr they at first made use of imitation (dummy) tanks on bicycle chassis (1925).

vehicle has two main military tasks: to provide a new type of weapon and to serve as a means of transport for men, guns and army needs. The combat vehicles grow into a special troop along with infantry, cavalry and artillery, without replacing any of them."

Since the results of World War I were unfortunate for both the Soviet Union and Germany, the two lands, out of common interests, signed the Treaty of Rapallo in 1922, followed by the Berlin Friendship Treaty of April 1924.

In the course of these agreements, though, there were were also secret talks for the purpose of military cooperation. This made it possible for the Germans to circumvent the Treaty of Versailles by testing military aircraft, poison gas and armored combat vehicles on Soviet territory. For tank testing, an artillery base with a training area and a firing range in the vicinity of Kazan (some 800 km east of Moscow) was chosen by retired Oberstleutnant

Malbrandt. The disguise name of this project, "Kama", was made of the first two letters of the names of Kazan and Malbrandt. It was obviously not noticed that the Kama river flowed into the Volga about a hundred miles south of Kazan. Thus the concealing value of the name was of little account.

After facilities for housing and service were built, the training courses and the testing of experimental vehicles could begin in the summer of 1929.

The German core personnel numbered some forty men, supported by 50 to 60 Russian assistants.

The most important goals were:

1. Testing available tank types, developing them further into "instruments usable in war", and training motor vehicle instructors and crews in all their functions.

2. Developing the most purposeful tank tactics, especially in the tactical terms of the platoon; determining the appropriate principles for movement and firing tactics.

3. Determining the most purposeful firing procedure, the firing principles and the possible effects.

4. Finding the best and quickest training methods for tank crews in short processes.

5. Developing ideas for antitank defense; organizing defenses and developing the necessary equipment.

Between 1929 and 1933, some thirty German and at least three times as many Soviet trainees were trained. These later formed a highly qualified instructional cadre for the training of each army's armored troops.

In the same period, tests of the German experimental vehicles "Grosstraktor", "Leichttraktor" and "Räder-Raupen-Kampfwagen M28" could be carried out. The last, another design by Vollmer under contract to the Gutehoffnung Steel firm, was the forerunner of the later tank produced by a Swedish affiliate as the "Landsverk 30", turned out in large numbers and offered for sale internationally.

With the breaking off of military cooperation in the autumn of 1933, about half a year after Hitler came to power, the "Kama" project was also ended. As its final result, the intensive testing on the Volga had saved the Germans long years of preliminary work which could not have been carried out in their own country before 1933-34. The fact that the first battle tanks could be put into series production in Germany in 1934 would have been impossible without Kama. Conceived like its forerunner, the "Grosstraktor", as a multiturreted combat vehicle, the Neubaufahrzeug originated in Germany in the 1932-1934 period, and a few of them saw service in Norway in April 1940.

At the end of the thirties the picture was very different: general overhaul of a Rheinmetall Neubaufahrzeug at the Borsigwalde works of the Altmärkisches Kettenwerk GmbH in 1939; in the background is the production line for the Panzer III tank.

Parallel to this, the following vehicles were developed, beginning in 1930:

- The **Kleintraktor** (1930-1932), also called LKA, LKB.

A further development was the Versuchs-Kfz. 617 test wagon; its disguised name for series production was "Landwirtschaftlicher Schlepper (LaS)" (= Agricultural Tractor) (1933-1935); it later became Panzerkampfwagen I.

- The **Zugführerwagen** (ZW) (1930-1936), or "Geschützkampfwagen 3.7 cm (Vs.Kfz. 619), later Panzerkampfwagen III, Type A.

- The **Bataillonsführerwagen** (BW) (1930-1936), also called Geschützkampfwagen 7.5 cm (Vs.Kfz. 618), later Panzerkampfwagen IV, Type A.

- The Vs.Kfz. 622 (1934-1936) in two different prototypes, the LaS 100 (MAN-Henschel) and LKA 2 (Krupp).

The first became the later Panzerkampfwagen II a1-a3.

These vehicles were in series production, constantly being made more combat-effective over the years, as the standard vehicles of the German Panzer troops, which were instituted on October 15, 1934, until well into World War II.

Their massive, surprising and mobile use was the basis for the success of the "Blitzkrieg" in the first two years of the war.

The secret beginnings of the German Panzer troops, though, took place in Russia, where armored vehicles could be developed and tested technically and tactically within the "Kama" project.

Deutsche PzKpfw- Entwicklungen (1916 - 1936)
(vereinfachte Darstellung)

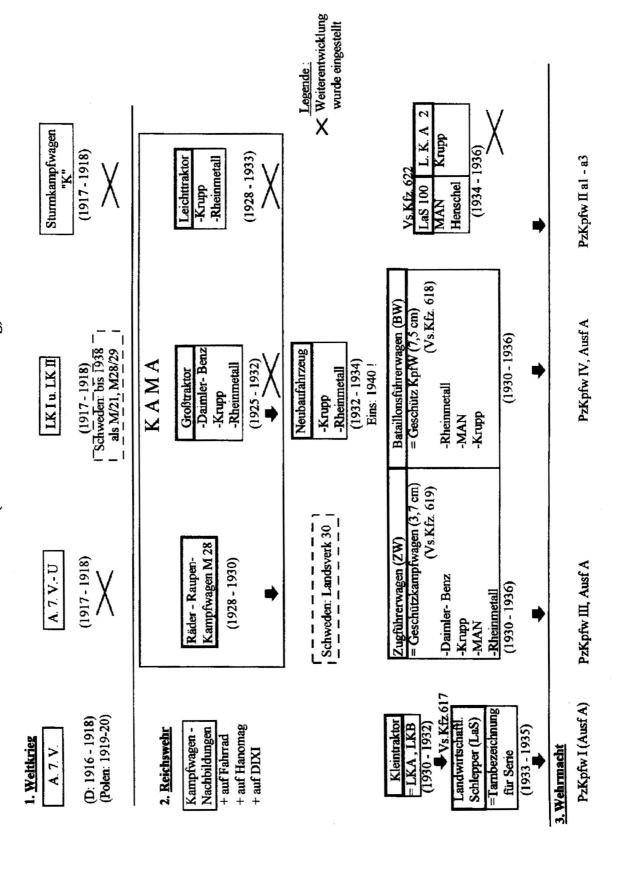

Legende :
✕ Weiterentwicklung wurde eingestellt

1. Weltkrieg

A. 7. V.

(D: 1916 - 1918)
(Polen: 1919-20)

A. 7 . V. - U

(1917 - 1918) ✕

LK I u. LK II

(1917 - 1918)
¯Schweden bis 1938¯
als M/21, M28/29

Sturmkampfwagen "K"

(1917 - 1918) ✕

2. Reichswehr

Kampfwagen - Nachbildungen
+ auf Fahrrad
+ auf Hanomag
+ auf DIXI

KAMA

Räder - Raupen- Kampfwagen M 28

(1928 - 1930) ➡

Großtraktor -Daimler- Benz -Krupp -Rheinmetall

(1925 - 1932) ✕

Leichttraktor -Krupp -Rheinmetall

(1928 - 1933) ✕

¯Schweden: Landsverk 30¯

Neubaufahrzeug -Krupp -Rheinmetall

(1932 - 1934)
Eins: 1940 !

Zugführerwagen (ZW) = Geschützkampfwagen (3,7 cm) (Vs.Kfz. 619)

-Daimler- Benz
-Krupp
-MAN
-Rheinmetall
(1930 - 1936)

Bataillonsführerwagen (BW) = Geschütz KpfW (7,5 cm) (Vs.Kfz. 618)

-Rheinmetall
-MAN
-Krupp
(1930 - 1936)

Kleintraktor = LKA , LKB

(1930 - 1932)
➡ Vs.Kfz.617

Landwirtschaftl. Schlepper (LaS) = Tambezeichnung für Serie

(1933 - 1935)

Vs.Kfz. 622		
LaS 100	L. K. A 2	
MAN	Krupp	
Henschel		

(1934 - 1936) ✕

3. Wehrmacht

PzKpfw I (Ausf A) ➡

PzKpfw III, Ausf A ➡

PzKpfw IV, Ausf A ➡

PzKpfw II a1 - a3 ➡

Origins

Sturmpanzerwagen A.7.U and A.7.V.-U

The first suggestion for the design of an off-road-capable combat vehicle was made by the Austrian Oberleutnant Burstyn in 1912.

But both the K.u.K. Austrian and the Prussian war ministries rejected this suggestion as technically impossible and tactically worthless.

In order to overcome the static situation in France during World War I, the British Navy suggested making a path for the infantry through wire barriers and trenches by using a "land ship" on tracks.

Under the strictest secrecy, construction tests wre carried out with tanks since 1915. Finally, 49 of the heavy Mark I tank were utilized as combat vehicles at the front for the first time by the British troops at Flers, 30 kilometers south of Arras, in the battle of the Somme.

After they had at first caused fear and panic among the German troops, the infantry and artillery soon zeroed in on their new adversary. At Cambrai, on November 20-21, 1917, about 107 of 474 enemy tanks were put out of action by direct fire from AA and artillery guns or by massed hand-grenade charges used by the infantry.

Only on November 13, 1916 did the German Army command decide to build battle tanks. Since only a few technical details were available despite the experience at the front, the technical commission given the task of designing them, under the direction of Oberingenieur Vollmer, had to find their own way in designing them.

Since a decision had been made in favor of straight tracks as the means of movement, a Holt tractor obtained from Austria served as a model.

In view of the original disagreement of the War Ministry as to the use of these vehicles, the form of the chassis was made universal:

1. As a battle tank with an armored body and

2. as a cross-country vehicle and towing tractor with a bed for transporting war materials and the like.

The grandfather of all German tanks, the Sturmpanzerwagen A.7.V. Twenty vehicles of this type were made. By the end of the war, they were opposed by some 2000 Allied tanks. The A.7.V. was armed with a 5.7 cm gun at the bow and six heavy machine guns, firing out of machine-gun mounts at the sides and rear. Other light weapons and devices were carried inside the vehicle. The crew consisted of 18 men, and deploying members of the crew during combat was very customary.

The driver's and commander's seats were situated above the powerplant, which was located in the geometrical center of the chassis. Below the seats, the two 100 HP Daimler motors were installed.

The armor of the vehicle consisted of 39 mm riveted steel plates at the front, 20 mm on the sides and 15 mm on top. As its main weapon the tank had a 5.7 cm Maxim Nordenfelt gun, mounted forward in the bow. One hundred shells with impact fuses (and delayers) were carried, plus forty armor-piercing shells and forty canister shells. In addition, the tank had six heavy machine guns, which fired out of machine-gun loopholes. The crew numbered eighteen and consisted of

1 commander (Leutnant),
2 drivers,
1 mechanic,
9 machine gunners,
3 artillerymen (gun crew),
1 signalman, and
1 messenger,

armed with eight machine guns, carbines, pistols, hand grenades and flamethrowers. During combat it was customary for some of the crew to get out and fight on foot. Despite numerous problems, the prototype had been finished by Daimler-Benz at the end of April 1917. Its name A.7.V. was that of the department responsible for its production (Allgemeines Kriegsdepartment, 7. Abteilung, Verkehrswesen). After successful test drives, the Army command issued contracts for 90 A.7.V. tanks, twenty of which—called "Sturmpanzerwagen" as of 1918—were to be built. Their production was delayed considerably, mainly by raw material shortages. Thus the twenty Sturmpanzer were only put into service on the western front in the spring of 1918, when the Allies already had more than 2000 tanks in action.

After the war ended, the German tanks had to be turned over to the Allies, who passed them on to Poland. Some A.7.V. Sturmpanzer are said to have been used in battle against Russia in 1920-21. Their fate is unknown.

Australian units captured the A.7.V. Sturmpanzerwagen "Mephisto" in 1918. The only original specimen still in existence, it is now in a museum at Brisbane, Australia. It served as a model for the German copy, which is now in the Panzermuseum in Munster.

Some 75 A.7.V. chassis were equipped with truck bodies and used as gun and ammunition tractors. These vehicles also proved themselves very well. Another design by Oberingenieur Vollmer, though, the A.7.V.-U, proved to be a complete failure. It was built on the model of the British Mark IV tank with external chain tracks and a gun balcony, but its prototype showed such serious defects that no further production was done.

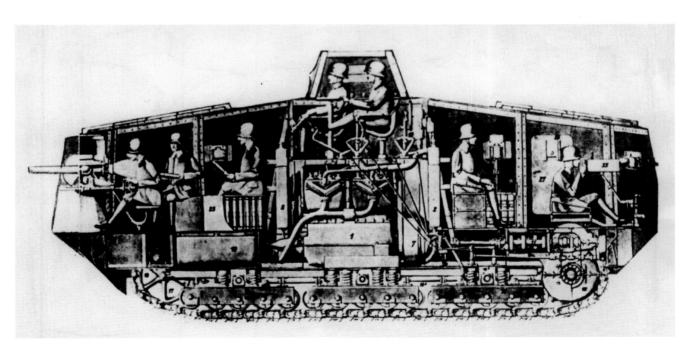

This cutaway drawing of the A.7.V. Sturmpanzerwagen shows the arrangement of its most important components, as well as the battle stations of the crew inside the vehicle. In the middle, above the powerplant, are the commander and driver; in the bow (left) is the three-man gun crew for the 5.7 cm gun. The other crewmen were carried either at the six machine-gun positions or in the accessible interior.

The prototype of the A.7.V.-U heavy tank. This design showed such serious faults that no further production was done. Its identifying marks, based on the British model, included the tracks that ran over the entire hull and the gun balcony mounted on the side.

Technical Data

	STURMPANZERWAGEN A.7.V.	STURMPANZERWAGEN A.7.V.-U
Motor	Daimler two, central, side by side	Daimler two, central, side by side
Cylinders	4 in-line each	4 in-line each
Displacement	17,000 cc each	17,000 cc each
Performance	100 HP each	150 HP each
Cooling	water	water
Gears	3 forward, 3 reverse	3 forward, 3 reverse
Running gear	under armor 1 rear drive wheel, 1 front road wheel, 3 trucks with 5 rollers each, coil springs	outside armor
Clearance	0.40 m	?
Ditch span	2.00 meters	?
Climbing	0.70 meter	?
Climbing %	16%	?
Overall length	7350 mm	8380 mm
Overall width	3100 mm	4690 mm
Overall height	3400 mm	3140 mm
Fighting weight	32.0 tons	39.0 tons
Crew	18 men	7 men
Armament	1 5.7 cm gun, 6 heavy MG	1 5.7 cm gun, 4 MG
Armor plate	front 30 mm, rear and sides 20 mm, top 15 mm other 20 mm	front 30 mm, all, side and other 20 mm
Top speed	12 kph	12 kph
Fuel capacity	2 x 250 liters (rear)	2 x 250 liters (rear)
Range	35 km	30 km

Light Battle Tanks
LK I and LK II

Vollmer represented the viewpoint that instead of fewer heavy tanks, a great number of light tanks should be built. Thus he developed, within a short span of time, the LK I, weighing about eight tons, on the basis of available chassis of heavy personnel vehicles. After his first failure to get the high Army command to accept his design, his concept was presented again and approved in September 1917.

It resembles the British "Whippet", with flat external running gear and high, turretlike rear bodywork.

At the very front of the chassis is the engine room, in which the radiator and the powerplant, a 55 HP 1910 model motor made by Benz, were installed. The driving power was carried from it through the gears, divider drive and shaft in the drive room to the drive wheel. The steering of the vehicle was done by two steering levers, which worled on two lamellar couplings on the driveshaft, by which the speeds of the two tracks could be regulated separately.

The fighting compartment, which was located above the drive room, was equipped with three doors, one on each side and one at the rear. Every door in turn was fitted with a hatch, and there were six more hatches in the walls, four at the front and one on each side. Every hatch was equipped with a peephole, in order to provide a view even when under fire.

In the manually rotating turret, an MG 08 or MG 08/15 was installed.

The LK II light tank was armed with a 3.7 cm gun and two water-cooled MG 08 or MG 08/15 machine guns. The 1912 model MG made by Steyr was also used. The radiator grille was placed on the upper side of the engine room, the bow of the vehicle was armored and made to overhang.

The construction of 800 of these vehicles was given the highest level of priority. The vehicles were to be finished by the spring of 1919. It was intended that they be used in units of three companies with thirty tanks each plus a staff with ten of them. Ten chassis of the LK II reached Sweden by secret means after the war ended (1921). To circumvent the terms of the Treaty of Versailles, they were exported to Sweden as agricultural materials and steam generator units for a total of 100,000 Kronen. The armor plate was as yet unhardened; a suitable hardening process still had to be developed in Sweden. In 1929 these vehicles, designated "stridsvagn m/21", were modernized as the m/29 version. The German motor was replaced by a 60 HP Scania-Vabis 1544 engine and a new gearbox was built. In addition, two headlights with folding shields were installed at the front. The fighting weight increased to 9.5 tons.

After further modifications and sixteen years of use, these vehicles were taken out of service in 1938. One vehicle of this type can be seen in the Panzermuseum in Munster.

The 800 planned light tanks never saw action with the troops. The LK I was armed with a machine gun (MG 08 or 08/15) in the turret and powered by a 55 HP Daimler-Benz gasoline engine.

Die vorgesehenen 800 Leichten Kampfwagen kamen nicht mehr zum Einsatz bei der Truppe. Der LK 1 war mit einem Maschinengewehr (MG 08 oder 08/15) im Drehturm und einem 55-PS-Daimler-Benz-Ottomotor ausgestattet.

Technical Data

	LK I	LK II
Motor		
	Daimler-Benz Otto	Daimler-Benz Otto
Cylinders	?	?
Displacement	?	?
Performance	55 HP	55 HP
Cooling	?	?
Gears	?	?
Running gear	exposed tracks	exposed tracks
Clearance	0.27 meter	0.27 meter
Ditch spanning	2.00 meters	2.00 meters
Climbing	0.45 meter	0.45 meter
Climbing gradient	41%	41%
Overall length	5080 mm	5060 mm
Overall width	1950 mm	1950 mm
Overall height	2520 mm	2520 mm
Fighting weight	8.0 tons	8.5 tons
Crew	3 men	3 men
Armament	2 machine guns	5.7 cm rapid-fire (one a spare) gun, later 3.7 cm Krupp tank gun, or 2 machine guns
Armor plate	14 mm except 8 mm top	14 mm except 8 mm top
Top speed	14 kph	14 kph
Fuel capacity	140 liters	140 liters
Range	70 kilometers	70 kilometers

Side view of the LK II Light Tank. This vehicle was armed with a 3.7 cm gun in a loophole and two machine guns in the high rear body. Ten LK II chassis were sold to Sweden, circumventing the terms of the Treaty of Versailles. There they were used in the army until 1938 as stridsvagn m/21 and later as m/29.

Large Battle Tank "K"

As a hybrid development that failed, and that much resembled the giant Maus tank of World War II, the overly heavy "K" tank was created on order of the Chief of Field Vehicles in the O.H.L. This gigantic vehicle, which was conceived as a cannon-proof breakthrough vehicle, had internal running gear with a long, broad balcony on each side. For railroad transport, these tanks had to be dismantled. Two prototypes were destroyed in 1918, shortly before they would have been finished.

Technical Data

Motors	2 gasoline
Cylinders	?
Displacement	?
Performance	2 x 650 HP
Cooling	water
Gears	?
Tracks	under armor plate
Total length	12,700 mm
Total width	3000 mm, with balconies 6000 mm
Total height	3000 mm
Fighting weight	150 tons
Crew	22 men
Armament	4 semi-automatic 77 mm rapid-fire guns and 7 7/92 cm machine guns
Armor plate	30 mm
Top speed	1.9-7.5 kph
Fuel capacity	?
Range	25 km

A model of the "K" heavy tank, almost 13 meters long, with the bow at right.

Another photo of a model of the "K" heavy tank. The vehicle, which was never finished, was to be armed with four 77 mm guns and seven machine guns.

Large Tractor

In May 1925 the Reich Defense Ministry issued contracts to the firms of Daimler, Krupp and Rheinmetall to develop and build two tanks each, weighing some sixteen tons. One year later the project was disguised with the name "Traktor", divided into the "Grosstraktor" (to 23 tons) and "Leichttraktor" (10-12 tons).

Technical Data

Fighting weight	16 tons
Outer dimensions	6500 x 2600 x 2400 mm
Top speed	40 kph
Climbing ability	1000 mm
Climbing gradient	45%
Spanning ability	2500 mm
Wading ability	800 mm
Swimming ability	By two screws, without any additional attachments, drive or steering
Armament:	
Main turret	7.5 cm gun L/24 (Vo 420 m/s) & 1 MG
Rear turret	1 machine gun
Bow	1 machine gun (added)
Crew:	
Bow	Commander (center), driver (left), radioman (right); commander was also machine gunner
Main turret	Aiming and loading gunners
Rear turret	Machine gunner (also operated propellers)
Armor plate	14 mm all around, steel-core bullet-safe
Gas safety	Prescribed
Powerplant	Aircraft engine, 250 HP at 1400 rpm

In addition, there were various non-standard components made by individual firms installed in the following parts:
-Variable gears
-Steering gear
-Running gear
-Suspension, and Tracks.

In 1925, developmental contracts for these vehicles were issued to the Rheinmetall and Krupp firms for a 7.5 cm tank gun and an antitank gun with high initial velocity.

The Krupp Grosstraktor on display at the barracks of Panzer Regiment 5 in Wünsdorf in 1937; note the turning machine-gun turret in the rear.

Special Features

The main turret was installed ahead of the central bulkhead, Behind the latter was the engine compartment, which was under high pressure, isolated and airtight. On the rear section of the rear body was a turning machine-gun turret.

To the left of the engine compartment was a crawl space between the fighting compartment and the machine-gun room, from which the motor could be serviced.

For getting in and out, there was a hatch at the right front of the vehicle, plus openings in the stroboscopes in the main turret, at the bottom of the rear machine-gun room, and in the roof of the machine-gun turret.

Above: This poor-quality picture is one of the few that show the Kama testing of the Grosstraktor.

Below: As on page 12, a Krupp Grosstraktor.

The Krupp Grosstraktor with three-color camouflage paint. Its armament consisted of a 7.5 cm gun and three heavy machine guns.

Production and Testing

While Krupp and Rheinmetall installed the BMW Va gasoline engine, which produced 250 HP at 1400 rpm, in their prototypes, Daimler used a former Daimler aircraft engine, now called Type D IV and able to produce 300 HP at 1400 rpm.

In the course of building the prototypes (1928), the equipping of the vehicles with radios and a bow machine gun was ordered.

While Krupp finished its vehicles at the firing range in Meppen, the Rheinmetall and Daimler Grosstraktors were assembled at the firing range in Unterlüss.

Since technical testing could not be done in Germany because of the terms of the Treaty of Versailles, all six prototypes were packed into crates and shipped in June 1929 via Leningrad to Kazan, where the secret "Kama" tank school had meanwhile been established. There, immediately after their arrival, driving and shooting tests were begun.

While Krupp and Rheinmetall had covered 63 and 133 kilometers by 1929, the two Daimler Grosstraktors' performance was insignificant, as it remained in the following years, so that they were no longer used after 1931.

The machine-gun turrets in the rear were removed at the end of 1929 to make access to the powerplant easier. In 1931-32 the Krupp vehicles were fitted with new ZF synchromesh (Aphon) variable gears. New steel-link tracks with central teeth were also put into use.

After a differential steering drive broke down in one of the Rheinmetall Grosstraktors, it was replaced by a Cletrac steering gear. In 1933-34 this was also installed in the second Rheinmetall vehicle. They, along with the Krupp vehicles, also received lubricated steel-link tracks. Instead of two groups of road wheels with eight small rollers each, new running gear with twelve bigger rollers, 320 mm in diameter, arranged in pairs, were installed in the Rheinmetall vehicles.

In August 1933 a discussion took place in Kazan concerning the further development of the Grosstraktor; the results were utilized later in the development of the Neubaufahrzeug tanks.

At first the political events in Germany seemed to have no influence on the work in Kazan. But after the absence of the Soviet trainees, orders came in July 1933 to close down the "Kama" project by September 15, 1933.

As a result, all the Gross- and Leichttraktor prototypes arrived in Stettin by September 21, 1933. The Grosstraktors were sent first to the Daimler-Benz firm in Berlin-Marienfelde to be prepared for their further use in the following year.

While the two Daimler-Benz Grosstraktors were set up as monuments at the headquarters of the newly formed German Panzer troops (Panzer Regiment 1 in Erfurt and 5 in Wünsdorf), as of April 1934 the driver training begun in Kazan in 1933 was continued on the peninsula of Wustrow, Mecklenburg, using the remaining Grosstraktors.

A Daimler-Benz heavy tractor, seen after being assembled in Unterlüss (Lüneburg Heath) and just before being shipped to Kazan, Russia.

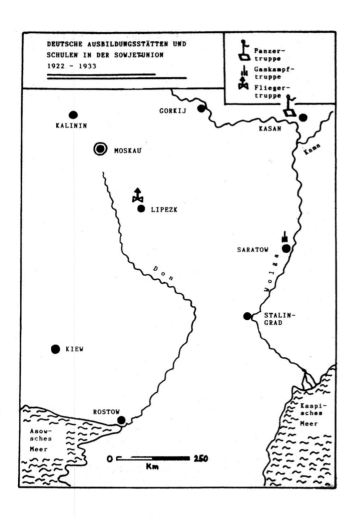

Panzer-
truppe
Gaskampf-
truppe
Flieger-
truppe

KALININ

GORKIJ

KASAN

MOSKAU

Kama

LIPEZK

Don

Volga

SARATOW

STALIN-
GRAD

KIEW

ROSTOW

Kaspi-
sches
Meer

Asow-
sches
Meer

0   250
Km

In the winter of 1934-35 the tractors were prepared at the Döberitz-Elsgrund training camp for the large Panzer test program at the Munster-Lager training camp in the summer of 1935. When this program was finished, both tractor types put in useful service for several years at the Panzer gunnery school in Putlos on the Baltic Sea, being used for training and testing.

One Grosstraktor set up as a monument in Putlos was dismantled and destroyed by the British after the war ended.

Left: German training facilities in the Soviet Union, 1922-1933.
Below: In front of the city of Kazan, barely recognizable on the horizon, is the Kama camp. The tall barracks buildings were used by the Russians; the German barracks are to the right. In Kazan, testing of the Grosstraktor, the Leichttraktor and the Räder-Raupen-Kampfwagen M28 was carried out.

This Daimler-Benz Grosstraktor, seen at the Löberfeld Barracks (of Panzer Regiment 1) in Erfurt, was also used as a display piece.

A Daimler-Benz Grosstraktor with a long (!) gun barrel, seen in Wünstorf. The further development of the Daimler-Benz vehicles was halted after the end of testing at Kazan (1933).

On this Daimler-Benz Grosstractor, the projecting bow machine-gun barrel amd the covered headlight in the center of the bow can be seen clearly.

A Rheinmetall Grosstraktor with off-road-type frame antenna and outboard-mounted tools on the sides. The headlight on the bow with its sensitive lens was fitted with a protective cover. In the bow were the seats of three crewmen: the commander in the middle, driver at left, radioman at right.

This Rheinmetall Grosstraktor was also put on display at the Panzer Troop School in Wünsdorf after testing at Kama. It was driven, as was the Krupp version, by a 250 HP VMW Va gasoline engine, originally designed as an aircraft engine.

Technical Data

	DAIMLER-BENZ G.T.I	KRUPP M. 18 Grosstraktor	RHEINMETALL GR. TR.
Motor	Daimler D IV b (aircraft motor)	BMW Va (aircraft motor)	BMW Va (aircraft motor)
Cylinders	6 in-line	6 in-line	6 in-line
Displacement	31,200 cc	22,920 cc	22,920 cc
Performance	255 HP	250 HP	250 HP
Cooling	Liquid	Liquid	Liquid
Variable gear	hydraulic planetary spring band pre-selector	Compressed air	Electric
Speeds fwd/rev.	3+ / 2	3+ / 2	4+ / 2
Track system	wheels/rollers	wheels/rollers	wheels/roll.
Track of tank	2220 mm	2200 mm	2230 mm
Track length	4000 mm	4000 mm	4250 mm
Track width	380 mm	370 mm	370 mm
Number of links	85	88	91
Suspension	Leaf springs	Coil springs	Coil springs
Ground clearance	400 mm	360 mm	410 mm
Spanning limit	2000 mm	2000 mm	2000 mm
Climbing limit	1000 mm	1000 mm	1000 mm
Climbing gradient	30 degrees	30 degrees	30 degrees
Overall length	6650 mm	6420 mm	6500 mm
Overall width	2780 mm	2760 mm	2600 mm
Overall height	2450 mm	2300 mm	2300 mm
Fighting weight	16.0 tons	16.4 tons	17.6 tons
Ground pressure	0.52 kg/cc	0.52 kg/cc	0/52 kg/cc
Crew	6	6	6
Armament, ammunition carried			
Primary	7.5 cm L/24, 100 rounds	7.5 cm L/24, 102 rounds	7.5 cm L/24, 104 rounds
Secondary	3 sMG, 6000	3 sMG, 6000	3 sMG, 6000
Armor plate			
Hull thickness	10-14 mm	10-14 mm	10-14 mm
Turret thickness	10 mm	10 mm	10 mm
Top speed	40 kph	37.5 kph	40 kph
Fuel capacity	400 liters	360 liters (150+105+105)	480 liters
Range	150 km	150 km	150 km

Front view of a Rheinmetall Grosstraktor. The opening for the bow machine gun, the covered headlight and the two cupolas for the driver and radioman are easy to see. Note the large mantle of the coaxial turret machine gun.

The Leichtraktor

In the summer of 1928, the general requirements for the development of a "Leichttraktor" were established. The vehicle was supposed to fulfill the following different tasks:
- Self-propelled mount for the 3.7 cm tank gun,
- Armored supply vehicle, and
- Tractor for light to medium loads.

Among other things, the following special requirements for the vehicle were established:
- 360-degree turntable with (semi-)automatic 3.7 cm gun and parallel heavy machine gun,
- Ammunition supply of at least 150 rounds for the tank gun and 3000 rounds for the heavy machine gun,
- Four crewmen,
- Sufficient armor against rifle and machine-gun bullets with steel cores,
- Average road speed of 25-30 kph,
- Climbing gradient of 30 degrees,
- Climbing and wading ability of 600 mm each,
- range of 150-200 kilometers,
- Specific ground pressure of 0.5 kilogram per square meter.

In conjunction with Krupp, Rheinmetall began the development of three test vehicles. They were equipped with Cletrac steering apparatus and 100 HP Daimler truck motors. The motor was installed in the bow of the vehicle; the fighting compartment was in the rear part of the tank. The commander and gunner had their places in the turret, the driver and radioman were housed in the hull. In addition to the two turret hatches, the vehicle had a rear door in the right part of the rear hull wall. On each side of the vehicle there were twelve road wheels, divided into three sets of four and sprung by leaf springs. The third vehicle (tank-destroyer version) was a self-propelled chassis armed with a 3.7 cm PaK L/45 and a light machine gun. Its crew consisted of only three men. The one-man turret was made considerably smaller.

The Leichttraktor of the Krupp firm used the same six-cylinder Daimler-Benz M36 gasoline engine as the Rheinmetall vehicles but differed particularly in its hull layout and running gear. While the bow of the Rheinmetall vehicle rose into a wedge shape, the Krupp Leichttraktor's body was stepped in about the center of the hull, in its transition from engine room to fighting compartment. There were basic differences in the running gear. Krupp used nine, Rheinmetall twelve rollers on each side. Krupp used coil springs in its suspension; Rheinmetall used leaf springs.

After the vehicles were finished in April and May 1930, two Leichttraktors of each firm were transported to the Kama training camp in Kazan, in the Soviet Union.

The Krupp Leichttraktor during testing in Kazan, Russia; note the design features of the running gear.

Side view of the Rheinmetall Leichttraktor armed with a 3.7 cm gun. This vehicle also has three-color camouflage paint. The running gear on each side consisted of the drive wheel at the front, the steering wheel at the back, and the twelve rollers in between, divided into three groups of four.

Since putting them to use involved no particular difficulties, they were able to cover much ground already in 1930.

In Kazan they were used to instruct trainees in the areas of technology, tactics and firing. Although they proved to be generally ready for action, the following shortcomings were noted:
- Unsatisfactory mobility,
- Insufficient cooling of the motor and steering gear,
- high wear of the lubricated track links.

Above: This diagonal view of the Rheinmetall Leichttraktor from the right rear clearly shows the two large open hatches on the rear sides of the turret and the open rear door on the right rear of the hull.

Below: The same vehicle with its gun barrel elevated.

The Rheinmetall Leichttraktor seen at an angle from the right front. Note the form of the exhaust pipe, the spiral shape of the muffler, the track apron over the rear half of the running gear, the frame antenna mounted on it, the two periscopes atop the turret, the boxy cupola for the driver ahead of the turret on the left, and the louvered engine cover.

As of January 1932, the Leichttraktor was equipped with new experimental tracks with and without rubber pads.

After the end of testing in the Soviet Union, all four vehicles returned to Germany in the autumn of 1933. There they were turned over to the Army Equipment Office in Spandau, which sent them on to the Panzer Gunnery School of Alt-Gaarz at Wustrow at the end of the year. Without any major treatment of their weak points, they were kept ready for tactical and firing training. In this role they remained extremely useful for a number of years.

The Rheinmetall Leichttraktor with opened engine covers and open driver's and radioman's hatches.

Another Rheinmetall Leichttraktor, but with completely new running gear. This vehicle was set up as a display piece at the troop training camp in Putlos at the end of the thirties.

The Panzerjäger version of the Rheinmetall Leichttraktor, with a smaller turret in which the commander assumed the duties of the gunner. The engine covers and the bow bodywork were also changed.

The Panzerjäger version with smooth engine covers, large air intakes in the bow plate, the latter crudely protected from ingesting large foreign bodies by a snakelike deflector. In the center ahead of the turret is the headlight, turned downward to the front; beside it is the boxy cupola for the driver, with its vision slit. On each side of the hull, above the tracks near the front, is a small headlight.

Angled view of the Rheinmetall Leichttraktor (Panzerjäger version), with closed rear door.

Technical Data

	Rheinmetall Leichttraktor	Krupp Leichttraktor
Motor	Daimler-Benz M36	Daimler-Benz M36
Cylinders	6 in-line	6 in-line
Displacement	7793 cc	7793 cc
Performance	100 HP	100 HP
Cooling	Liquid	Liquid
Variable gear	ZF Aphon	ZF Aphon
Speeds fwd./rev.	4/1 + supplementary	4/1 + supplementary
Running gear	Road & return wheels	Road & return wheels
Track of vehicle	1800 mm	1810 mm
Track length	2740 mm	2580 mm
Track width	270 mm	270 mm
Links per track	72	72
Suspension	Leaf springs	Coil springs
Ground clearance	290 mm	305 mm
Spanning ability	1000 mm	1000 mm
Climbing ability	270 mm	270 mm
Climbing gradient	30 degrees	30 degrees
Overall length	4320 mm	4350 mm
Overall width	2260 mm	2370 mm
Overall height	2270 mm	2350 mm
Fighting weight	8.96 tons	8.7 tons
Ground pressure	0.73 kg/sq.cm.	0.73 kg/sq.cm.
Crew	4	4
Armament, ammunition		
Primary	3.7 cm L/45, 150	3.7 cm L/45, 150
Secondary	machine gun, 3000	machine gun, 3000
Armor (hull & turret)	13 mm all around	13 mm all around
Top speed	35 kph	37 kph
Fuel capacity	110 liters	140 liters
Range	150 km	150 km

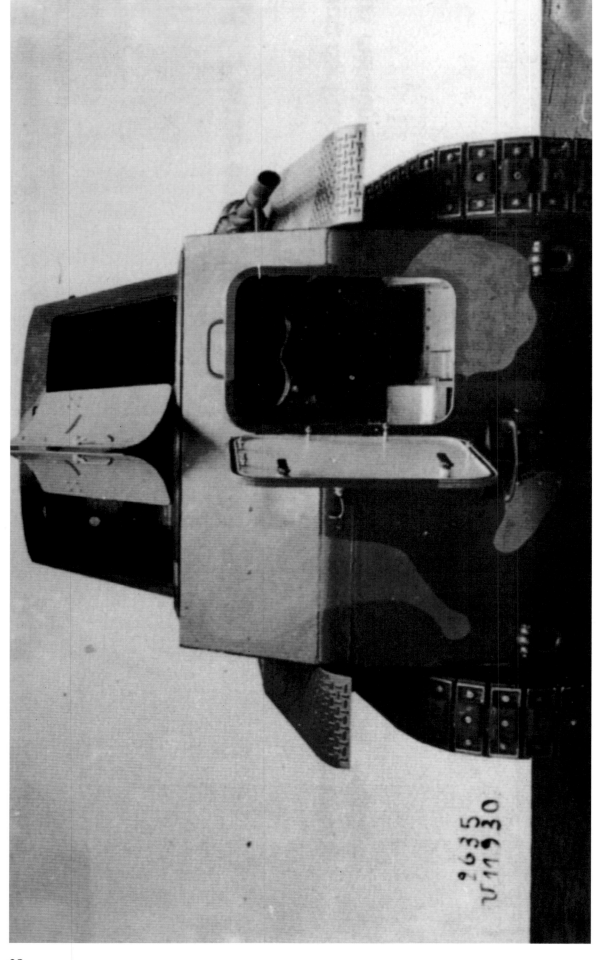

Rear view of the Panzerjäger version; note the two opened turret hatches and the rear door, which opens to the left, affording a view into the interior. Other interesting details are the exhaust tailpipe over the right track apron, the trailer hitch under the opened rear door, and the two towing eyes at the corners of the rear wall.

Räder-Raupen Kampfwagen M 28

In the latter half of the twenties, it was thought that the problems of track drive could be cured by a switchable running gear, so that one could let the vehicle run on wheels on paved roads and streets, and use the tracks off the road. Thus Dipl.-Ing. O. Merker, under contract to the Gutehoffnungshütte, began in 1928 to develop a light tank with switchable running gear for the Swedish branch firm of Landsverk.

Of the total of six vehicles designated "Räder-Raupen-Kampfwagen M 28" (or GFK) and built by the Gutehoffnungshütte, one vehicle was used at the Kama test center beginning in 1930. Here the vehicle proved to be underpowered, and the running gear turned out to be overburdened.

The motor was mounted at the left front, with the driver's seat beside it on the right. The vehicle was fitted with an additional seat for the backward driver at the other end of the chassis. Test vehicles 1 to 3 were equipped with a 50 HP 4-cylinder Benz gasoline engine, vehicles 4 to 6 with a 70 HP 4-cylinder NAG D7 gasoline engine.

The hind wheels were driven by chains. The suspension for the use of the tracks consisted of semi-elliptic springs, and that for the wheels used flap springs. The track drive consisted of two roller trucks on each side, each with four rollers on a half-spring, and one truck with two rollers on a flap spring.

The steel disc wheels were shod with puncture-proof tires.

Test vehicles 1 to 4 had an electric, vehicles 5 and 6 a hydraulic lifting apparatus to change from wheel to track drive. The process took place automatically in about 50 seconds.

If necessary, the change could be made manually by four men in about five minutes. The turret was equipped with a fully automatic 3.7 cm gun and a 7.9 mm Dreyse machine gun; the alternate driver also had a machine gun. The principle of a tank with switchable running gear was not pursued any more in Germany.

The further development of the Räder-Raupen-Kampfwagen was done from 1929 on by the Swedish branch firm of Landsverk and led to the production, beginning in 1931, of the Landsverk 30 and Landsverk 80 series vehicles.

The Räder-Raupen-Kampfwagen M28 of the Gutehoffnungshütte, running on wheels. This relatively small vehicle had a four-man crew (commander, gunner, forward and backward drivers). Its armament consisted of a fully automatic 3.7 cm tank gun and two 7.9 mm machine guns (turret and rear). When it ran on wheels, the rear wheels were driven by chains.

The person in the foreground gives a good idea of the size. Inside the vehicle it must have been quite cramped. For track drive, as demonstrated here, the wheels—depending on the version of the vehicle—were lifted by an electric or hydraulic lifting apparatus.

This rear view of the Räder-Raupen-Kampfwagen allows a view of the arrangement of the switchable running gear. Set close to the hull walls are the narrow tracks, while the puncture-proof wheels are mounted farther out. In between is the lifting and lowering apparatus to change the type of drive used. Inside the wheels are the chains that drive them.

Front view of the GHH-M28 Räder-Raupen-Kampfwagen with its wheels down. On the right of the turret is the cupola for the forward driver, above it the 3.7 cm tank gun, and beside it the 7.9 mm turret machine gun.

The same vehicle running on tracks. Both the overhanging armored wall and the turret are made of riveted armor plates. At the left on the bow plate is the oval air intake for the 52 or 77 HP powerplant.

Technical Data

	M 28/GFK Benz version	M 28/GFK Büssing version
Motor	Benz	NAG D7
Cylinders	4 in-line	4 in-line
Displacement	4160 cc	3620 cc
Performance	52 HP	77 HP
Cooling	Liquid	
Variable gear	ZF K 45	
Track running gear	Road wheels & rollers	
Track of vehicle	1400 mm	
Track length	3120 mm	
Links per track	66	
Suspension	Semi-elliptic	
Running gear	Sheet steel hubs	
Tire size	975x225 / 36x8	
Track of vehicle	2360 mm	
Wheelbase	2800 mm	
Ground clearance	150 mm	
Spanning ability	?	
Climbing ability	?	
Climbing gradient	?	
Overall length	4380 mm	
Overall width	2600 mm	
Height minus upper body	1480 mm (on wheels)	
Fighting weight	7.0 tons	
Ground pressure	0.85 kg/sq. meter	
Crew	4	
Armament (ammunition)		
Primary	3.7 cm gun (200)	
Secondary	two 7.9 mm MG, NG 13 (Dreyse)	
Armor plate	?	
Top speed		
On treads	23 kph	
On wheels	46 kph	
Fuel capacity	70 liters	85 liters
Range		
On treads	80 km	
On wheels	180 km	

Left: The principle of switching running gear was followed up by the Swedish branch firm of Landsverk. This Landsverk 30 is running on tracks.

The Swedish Landsverk 30 running on wheels. Note the central lifting apparatus to change the type of running gear.

Neubaufahrzeug

As in Britain and the Soviet Union, the development of multi-turreted tanks was carried out in Germany. The tests at the Kama test center resulted in enthusiasm for the building of a "Newbuilt Vehicle" which was sometimes known (in addition to other names) as a "Medium Tractor". Although attempts were made, for the sake of competition, to involve as many firms as possible, only the Krupp and Rheinmetall firms declared that they were ready to develop and complete this tank. An appropriate contract was issued to each firm on October 25, 1932. According to it, Rheinmetall was to develop a vehicle with a 15-ton fighting weight, while Krupp's type could weigh 22 tons—to provide required protection against 3.7 cm shells. The main turret was to be armed with a 7.5 cm tank gun, which might be replaced by a 5 cm gun later.

In the Neubaufahrzeug, the BMW Va aircraft engine already used in the Grosstraktor was installed. This was started either by compressed air or by a hand crank.

The ZF SFG 280 variable gear had six forward speeds (2nd to 6th gears synchronized) and one reverse gear.

The Rheinmetall version was equipped with a Cletrac (double differential) steering gear, the Krupp vehicle with a mechanical Wilson steering gear.

The rear engine moved the vehicle via side shafts. The running gear consisted of the rear drive wheel on each side, ten rollers arranged in pairs, the leading wheel at the front, and another unsprung road wheel inserted between the leading wheel and the first rollers.

The 7.5 cm and 3.7 cm gun barrels had a common breech. Since the gun barrels of the Krupp vehicles were

The Neubaufahrzeug was a three-turret tank with 7.5 and 3.7 cm guns in the main turret and two machine-gun turrets. The Krupp Neubaufahrzeug shown here had the two guns mounted parallel to each other in the main turret. The crew of the Neubaufahrzeug numbered six men (commander, aiming gunner, loader, two machine gunners and driver).

The Krupp Neubaufahrzeug at an auto show in Berlin in 1939. Here the turret machine gun to the right of the main gun, and the machine gun of the same type in the front MG turret, can be seen clearly.

The running gear of both Neubaufahrzeug versions was identical and consisted of the drive wheel (rear), the leading wheel (front), and eleven rollers plus four return rollers; the suspension was by coil springs, and the tracks consisted of 118 links.

equipped with a vertical breech, the installation of the two guns side by side in the main turret was necessary. The gun barrels of the Rheinmetall version, on the other hand, could be installed one above the other because of their lateral breech-blocks. In addition, the main turret was armed with either an MG 13 or a new EMG 34 uniform machine gun.

The vehicles were equipped with a radio set, an on-board communication system and an electrical turret-turning apparatus.

From 1934 on the Neubaufahrzeug was subjected to driving tests at the Rheinmetall firing range in Unterlüss.

The six-man crew was made up of:
- three men on the main turret (commander, aiming gunner and loader),
- one machine gunner in each MG turret, and
- the driver at the left front.
The following hatches were provided:
- on the left wall of the turret

The Krupp Neubaufahrzeug with the guns in the main turret side by side.

The Rheinmetall Neubaufahrzeug with the guns in the main turret one above the other.

- at right in the front machine-gun turret,
- in the driver's cupola, and
- in the hull below the rear machine-gun turret.

Of the total of five completed vehicles (delivered early in 1936), the three Krupp vehicles were made of armor steel and the two Rheinmetall specimens of cast iron.

The Neubaufahrzeug was hard to manage because of the large crew and the problems of coordinating the multiple turrets; it also had an underpowered and unsuitable powerplant and running gear that no longer represented the technical potential of the times.

The vehicles were used for training at the Putlos gunnery school. The three Krupp Neubaufahrzeug vehicles (Fz 3-5) saw action in World War II in April 1940.

Above: Rheinmetall Neubaufahrzeug overhaul at the Borsigwalde works in 1939.

Below: A Krupp Neubaufahrzeug in the Oslo area in 1940. Behind it is a small command car on the PzKpfw 1 chassis.

The Krupp Neubaufahrzeug in action in Norway. The machine guns for the main turret and the front MG turret have not been installed. The crewman standing on top has his right foot on the driver's hatch. The two-piece commander's hatch is open.

Technical Data

Neubaufahrzeug (Rheinmetall & Krupp)

Motor	BMW Va
Cylinders	6 in-line
Displacement	22920 cc
Performance	250 HP
Cooling	Liquid
Gearbox	ZF SFG 280
Speeds fwd/rev	6/1
Running gear	road & return rollers
Track of tank	2390 mm
Track length	4460 mm
Track width	380 mm
Links	118
Suspension	Coil spring
Ground clearance	450 mm
Spanning ability	2200 mm
Climbing ability	1000 mm
Climbing gradient	30 degrees
Overall length	6650 mm
Overall width	3000 mm
Overall height	2900 mm
Fighting weight	19.5 tons
Ground pressure	0.58 kg/sq. cm
Crew	6
Armament (ammunition)	
Primary	7.5 cm L/24 gun (75)
Secondary	3.7 cm gun (37), 3 MG (6000)
Armor plate	
Hull (forward)	20 mm
Hull (sides/aft)	13 mm
Turret (all)	15 mm
Top speed	30 kph
Fuel capacity	240 + 217 = 457 liters
Range	120 km

Left: The vehicle's three turrets are shown clearly here. The main turret rises high above the two smaller machine-gun turrets.

Below: The front of the Krupp Neubaufahrzeug with the side-by-side guns, the turret MG in a ball mantlet, and the machine gun in a roller mantlet in the front turret.

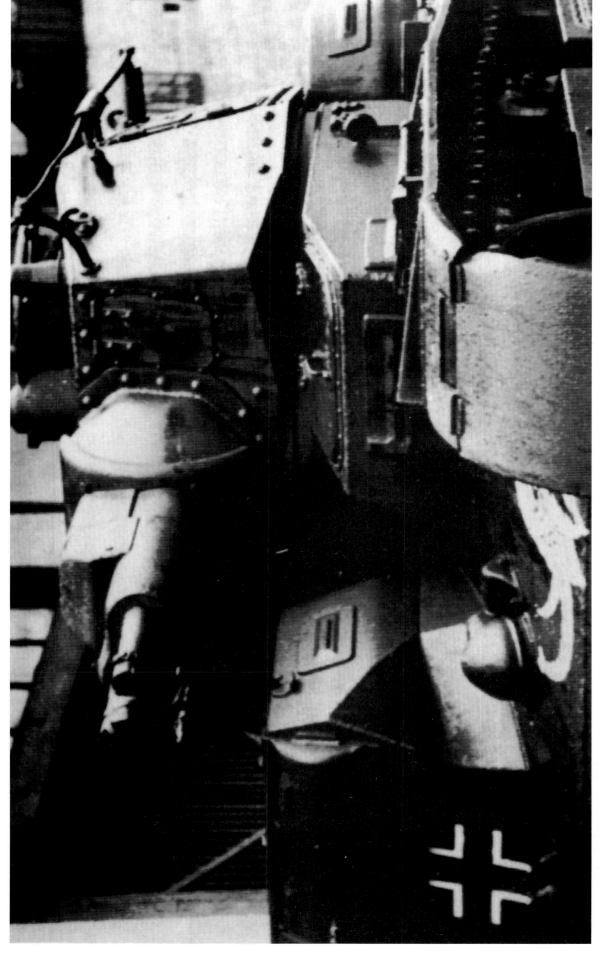

In this Krupp Neubaufahrzeug the rod antenna, folded forward, is mounted high on the left side of the turret, the closed driver's hatch (left ahead of the turret) and the folded-down headlight in the center of the bow are easy to see. Note the unusual position of the German cross on the front, here under the front machine-gun turret.

Development

The tests carried out in connection with the "Kama" undertaking showed clearly that new paths had to be followed in tank design, since both the Leicht- and the Grosstraktor, as well as the later Neubaufahrzeug, did not live up to the military requirements in terms of tactics and technology. To stand a chance on the battlefield against enemies with modern equipment, the design features for the later Panzerkampfwagen III and IV were already being determined at that time.

But since these vehicles could not be ready for series production before 1935-36 and the Army needed to have equipment for training available immediately on the enlargement of its ranks, it was decided to begin by developing a light tank, weighing some five to six tons, and armed with nachine guns.

KLEINTRAKTOR / AGRICULTURAL TRACTOR
Pz.-Kpfw. (M.G.)
KRUPP KLEINTRAKTOR WITH FRONT ENGINE

The design for a "Kleintraktor" presented by the Krupp firm in the autumn of 1930 was a full-track vehicle with a total weight of about 3.5 tons. It consisted of the chassis and a body including a turning turret and a 2 cm "machine cannon". In the front of the hull was the motor, along with the clutch and gearbox, and in the rear was the steering system, as well as the lateral shafts. Since this vehicle was also intended to serve as a towing tractor, the front-mounted engine allowed a better weight distribution, and at the same time the location of the gunner, who had to sit well to the rear on account of the long-barreled 2 cm weapon, was not interfered with. In 1932 a Kleintraktor prototype was finished and subjected to thoroughgoing tests. Further modifications did not take place, and the development was halted in mid-1933.

KLEINTRAKTOR WITH REAR ENGINE

In the autumn of 1931, front drive and rear engine were required in a light tank for the first time. The external measurements of the Kleintraktor that was already developed were to be retained, though. In the summer of 1932 the Inspector of Motorized Troops urged the hastened development of this vehicle for the ordered establishment of an initial tank company. At the end of July 1932 plans were on hand, including machine guns in place of the 2 cm turret weapon. In October 1932 the requested design work for the installation of a 2 cm gun was postponed. Because of the short [p. 43] time involved, the Krupp firm suggested, among other things, that the turret be fitted with twin machine guns.

In June 1933 a contract for the construction of four Kleintraktors at a price of 38,118.90 Reichsmark was received by the Krupp firm.

While the development designation of LKA or LKA was used by Krupp, the Army Weapons Office introduced the disguise name of "Landwirtschaftlicher Schlepper" (LaS) for the Kleintraktor in July 1933.

The chassis of the Krupp Kleintraktor with front drive and rear engine.

For the planned delivery of the first 150 LaS chassis, the Krupp firm named the period from December 31, 1933 to May 25, 1934. In order to put production on a broader basis, the firms of Rheinmetall, Daimler-Benz, MAN and Henschel were to handle some of the series production.

Above: The Krupp Kleintraktor chassis with added weight and traverse to minimize torsion.

Below: Chassis of the Agricultural Tractor (LaS), as the vehicle was called for troop testing.

a. bow armor, b. antenna, c. roller mantlet, d. turret, e. armored hull, f. rear armor

Test vehicle (Vs.Kfz.) 617, later designated PzKpfw I, Type A: a. bow armor, b. antenna, c. roller mantlet, d. turret, e. armored hull, f. rear armor.

For reasons of production and price, the Krupp firm declined the suggestion to equip part of the production run (135 units) of the Agricultural Tractor with a stronger motor. Instead, Krupp recommended carrying out parallel tests using a test vehicle with the more powerful motor.

After the assembly of the chassis was begun as planned, the first vehicle was finished on March 2, 1934. Three vehicles were turned over to the Army Weapons Office on April 27, 1934.

Krupp of Essen transferred production of the vehicles to the Krupp-Gruson Works in Magdeburg.

The Agricultural Tractor (LaS) was produced in the following series:

Krupp-Gruson:
Series 1: 135; Series 2: 100; Series 3: 215; Series 4: ?
Rheinmetall:
Series 1: 50; Series 2: 60; Series 3: ?; Series 4: ?
Daimler-Benz:
Series 1: 50; Series 2: 65; Series 3: ?; Series 4: ?
Henschel:
Series 1: 50; Series 2: 100; Series 3: 150; Series 4: 35
MAN:
Series 1: 50; Series 2: 110; Series 3: ?; Series 4: ?

The finished vehicles were delivered to the troops under the designation of "Pz.-Kpfw. (M.G.) - Sd. Kfz. 101, Ausf. A". They formed the nucleus of the newly established armored units.

The further development of this vehicle, which was used by the troops from 1935 on with the designation "Pz.-Kpfw. I (M.G.) - Sd. Kfz. 101, Ausf. B", included the installation of the Maybach 6-cylinder NL-38 carburetor engine. The larger motor made it necessary to lengthen the armored hull. This was done by adding a pair or road wheels. The leading wheels at the rear were now raised and an improved variable gear (ZF Aphon FG 31) was installed. Through these measures, the vehicle's capabilities were inproved, though its total weight was increased to six tons.

PzKpfw I, Type A: a. armored hull, b. rear armor, c. front armor, d. mounting positions, e. turret, f. antenna protector, g. antenna.

Technical Data

	Pz.-Kpfw. (M.G.), Sd.Kfz. 101, Type A	Pz.-Kpfw. I (M.G.), Sd.Kfz. 101, Type B
Motor	Krupp M 305	Maybach NL-38 TR
Cylinders	4 opposed	6 in-line
Displacement	3460 cc	3790 cc
Performance	57 HP	100 HP
Cooling	Air	Liquid
Gearbox	ZF FG 35	ZF FG 31
Speeds fwd/rev.	5 / 1	5 / 1
Running gear	Road wheels & return rollers	Road wheels & return rollers
Track of vehicle	1670 mm	1670
Track length	2470 mm	2470 mm
Track width	280 mm	280 mm
Number of links	84	100
Suspension	Leaf springs	Leaf springs
Ground Clearance	290 mm	290 mm
Spanning ability	1400 mm	1400 mm
Climbing gradient	30 degrees	30 degrees
Overall length	4020 mm	4420 mm
Overall width	2060 mm	2060 mm
Overall height	1720 mm	1720 mm
Fighting weight	5.4 tons	6.0 tons
Ground pressure	0.40 kg/sq. cm.	0.42 kg/sq. cm.
Crew	2	2
Armament (ammunition)		
Primary	none	none
Secondary	2 7.9 mm MG (1525) MG 13k	2 7.9 mm MG (1525) MG 13k
Armor plate	13 mm all around	13 mm all around
Top speed	37 kph	40 kph
Fuel capacity	145 liters	145 liters
Range on road	145 km	140 km
Range off road	97 km	115 km

PzKpfw I, Type B: The chassis was lengthened and given a fifth road wheel to make room for the more powerful 100 HP Mayback motor. The leading wheel at the rear was raised and a fourth return roller added.

Zugführerwagen Batallion Führerwagen (BW)

On the basis of the experience that had been gained in the "Kama" undertaking, it was obviously necessary to develop completely new concepts in tanks for the final equipping of the future German Panzer troops. Thanks to those who worked with Generaloberst Heinz Guderian, the order of priority of firepower, mobility and armor protection was established for the tactical requirements of tanks. In addition, the tasks of the crew members were now divided practically into the functions of the commander, aiming and loading gunners, driver and radioman. Beyond that, Guderian stressed the importance of equipping tanks extensively with means of communication.

For the "final equipping" of the Panzer troops, the Army Weapons Office required two basic types of armored combat vehicles:
- The tank armed with a 3.7 cm gun (Vs. Kfz. 619), with the disguise name of ZUGFÜHRERWAGEN (ZW) or Platoon Leader's Car.
- The tank armed with a 7.5 cm gun (Vs. Kfz. 618), with the disguise name of BATAILLONSFÜHRERWAGEN (BW) or Battalion Leader's Car.

While the Army Weapons Office foresaw the ZW as being armed with a 3.7 cm tank gun, the Inspection of Motorized Troops called for a 5 cm gun. For reasons of uniformity—the infantry was already equipped with the 3.7 cm PaK—the installation of the more powerful weapon was dropped for the time being, but the turret turning ring of the ZW was already laid out for the later inclusion of the 5 cm tank gun.

The turning turret developed by the firm of rheinmetall-Borsig held a 3.7 cm tank gun with a muzzle velocity of 760 meters per second. To the right of it were two MG 34 in a separate mantlet. The dependable cupola of the Neubaufahrzeug was installed in both vehicles as the commander's cupola.

The battalion leader's car was armed with a 7.5 cm caliber gun, as used in the Grosstraktor and the Neubaufahrzeug.

Before the end of 1934 the development contracts for both armored vehicles (15- and 18-ton classes) were issued by the Army Weapons Office to the firms of MAN, Daimler-Benz, Rheinmetall-Borsig and Krupp.

The powerplant was intended to be the water-cooled Maybach Type HL 108 V-12 gasoline engine, producing 300 HP, or its predecessor, the Type HL 100. The gearbox to be used was the ZF six-speed Synchron SSG 75 type.

In the development of the battalion leader's car, Rheinmetall-Borsig was in competition with the Krupp firm. After extensive testing, the Krupp version was chosen for production, with some features taken from the Rheinmetall design. Because of the urgency of the project, Daimler-Benz was contracted with for the series production of the platoon leader's car. The turret, though, was built by Rheinmetall-Borsig. With the platoon and battalion leaders' cars, the subsequent Panzerkampfwagen III and IV, the young German Panzer troops received tanks of the most modern type.

These vehicles did not reach the troops until 1936.

The Krupp prototype (MKA) of a medium battle tank, which was to be built in two versions as the Zugführerwagen (ZW) and Bataillonsführerwagen (BW).

The Rheinmetall prototype of the tank with a 7.5 cm gun, the Vs.Kfz. 618, with the disguise name of "Bataillonsführerwagen" (BW). This prototype already had the angled front body of the later first series production run, the PzKpfw. IV, Type A.

A pre-production version of the Zugführerwagen (Vs.Kfz. 619), this being the daimler-Benz type. This vehicle was armed with a 3.7 cm tank gun and three machine guns (two parallel ones at right in the mantlet, and one in a ball mantlet to the right of the driver). Unlike the following versions, the first production run of PzKpfw III, Type A, had the five large road wheels on each side, as hsown here.